WORLD OF WONDER
WOW
WORLD OF WONDER

THE AWESOME BOOK OF

VOLCANOES

Get ready to hear your kids say, "Wow! That's awesome!" as they dive into this fun, informative, question-answering series of books! Students—and teachers and parents—will learn things about the world around them that they never knew before!

This approach to education seeks to promote an interest in learning by answering questions kids have always wondered about. When books answer questions that kids already want to know the answers to, kids love to read those books, fostering a love for reading and learning, the true keys to lifelong education.

Colorful graphics are labeled and explained to connect with visual learners, while in-depth explanations of each subject will connect with those who prefer reading or listening as their learning style.

This educational series makes learning fun through many levels of interaction. The in-depth information combined with fantastic illustrations promote learning and retention, while question and answer boxes reinforce the subject matter to promote higher order thinking.

Teachers and parents love this series because it engages young people, sparking an interest and desire in learning. It doesn't feel like work to learn about a new subject with books this interactive and interesting.

This set of books will be an addition to your home or classroom library that everyone will enjoy. And, before you know it, you, too, will be saying, "Wow! That's awesome!"

"People cannot learn by having information pressed into their brains. Knowledge has to be sucked into the brain, not pushed in. First, one must create a state of mind that craves knowledge, interest, and wonder. You can teach only by creating an urge to know." - Victor Weisskopf

© 2012 Flowerpot Press

Contents under license
from Aladdin Books Ltd.

Flowerpot Press
142 2nd Avenue North
Franklin, TN 37064

Flowerpot Press is a
division of Kamalu, LLC,
Franklin, TN, U.S.A.,
and Mitso Media, Inc.,
Oakville, ON, Canada.

ISBN 978-1-77093-778-9

Illustrators:
Ian Thompson
Peter Roberts -
Allied Artists
Jo Moore

American Edition Editor:
Johannah Gilman Paiva

Designer:
Flick Killerby

American Redesign:
Jonas Fearon Bell

Printed in China.

CONTENTS

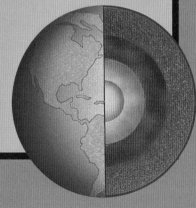

INTRODUCTION

Did you know that most volcanoes are under the sea? That volcanologists are volcano scientists? That the biggest volcano is on Mars?

Discover for yourself amazing facts about Earth's volcanoes and the people who study them. Learn about tsunamis, hot springs, black smokers, and volcanoes of the past—and in space.

Look out for this symbol, which means there is a fun project for you to try.

True or False? Watch for this symbol and try to answer the question before reading on for the answer.

ON THE SURFACE

The Earth's crust is made of pieces called "plates." These don't join up neatly—some overlap, and there are gaps between others. Volcanoes and earthquakes usually happen at fault lines, where the edges of plates move apart or grate together.

Copy the map of the Earth below, or enlarge it on a photocopier. Color it in, then cut along the fault lines. Can you fit all the plates back together? Can you find the Pacific Ocean plate? There are so many volcanoes around this plate that the area is called the "Ring of Fire."

Most earthquakes are not even noticeable, but about every three years there is a violent one somewhere in the world. In 1970, an earthquake in Peru made roads crack and buildings collapse. It caused a massive landslide—and 66,000 deaths.

The San Andreas Fault in California, on the West coast, is where two plates are sliding past each other in opposite directions. There have been many big earthquakes along this line. Even so, many people make their home there.

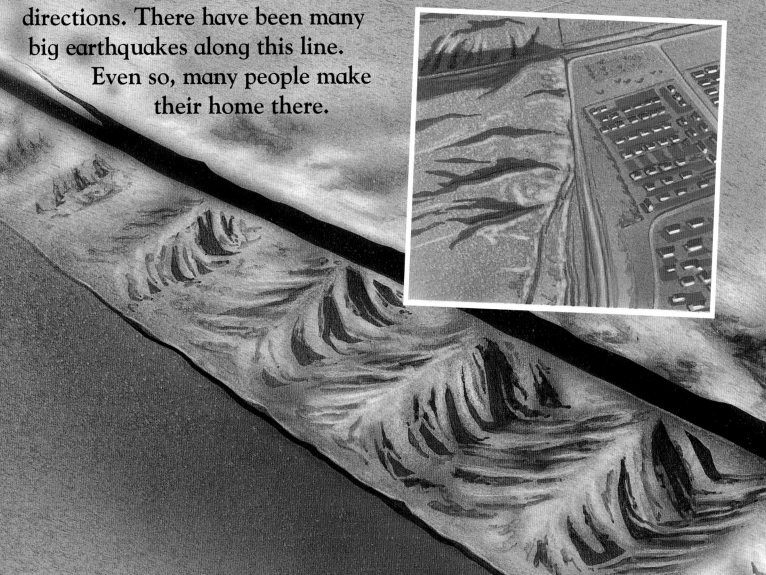

CRACKING UP

Volcanoes are openings in the Earth's crust, often on a fault line. Rock below the Earth's surface can get so hot it forms magma. When the pressure rises, it blasts a hole and the hot melted rock, ash, and gas escape.

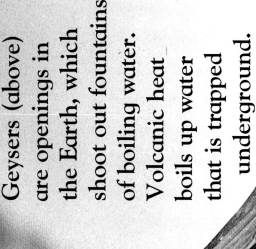

Geysers (above) are openings in the Earth, which shoot out fountains of boiling water. Volcanic heat boils up water that is trapped underground.

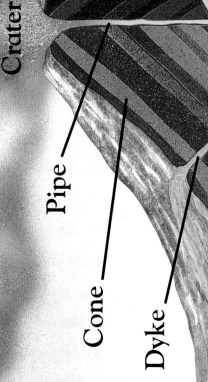

Crater

Pipe

Cone

Dyke

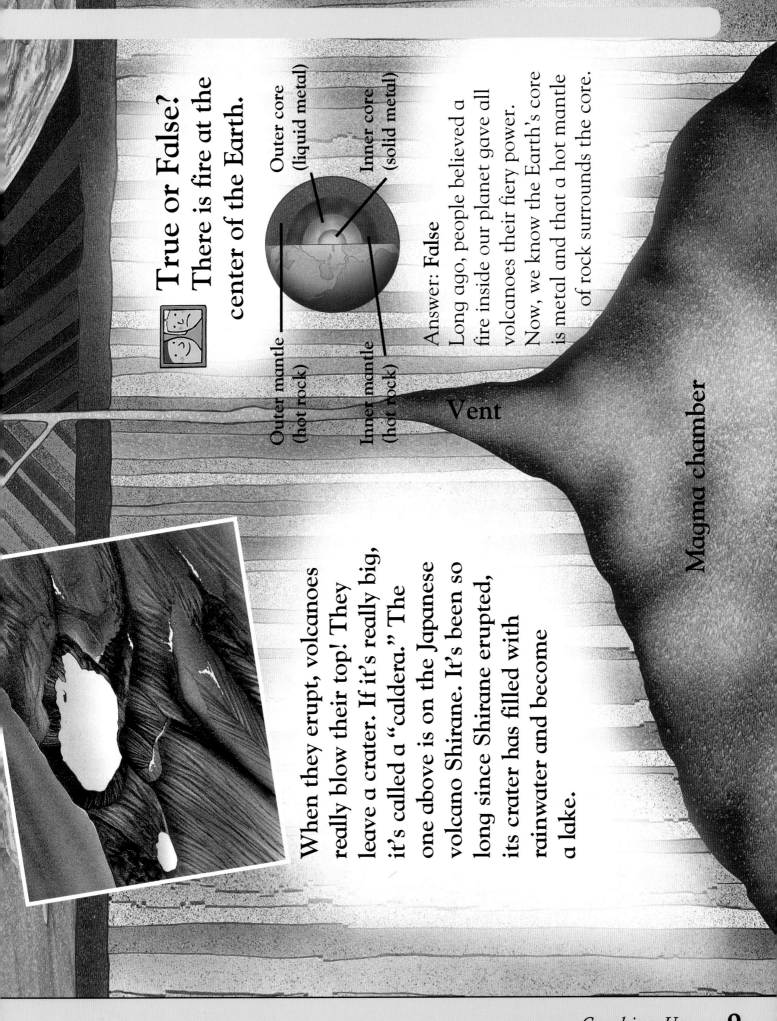

True or False?
There is fire at the center of the Earth.

Outer core (liquid metal)

Inner core (solid metal)

Outer mantle (hot rock)

Inner mantle (hot rock)

Answer: False
Long ago, people believed a fire inside our planet gave all volcanoes their fiery power. Now, we know the Earth's core is metal and that a hot mantle of rock surrounds the core.

Vent

Magma chamber

When they erupt, volcanoes really blow their top! They leave a crater. If it's really big, it's called a "caldera." The one above is on the Japanese volcano Shirane. It's been so long since Shirane erupted, its crater has filled with rainwater and become a lake.

RIVERS OF ROCK

When a volcano erupts, it squirts out hot, liquid rock called "lava." Sometimes the lava is thick and just oozes out. Sometimes the lava is so runny it gushes in rivers, flowing at speeds up to 14 miles (50 kilometers) per hour.

When a volcano shoots lava into the air, it makes a fountain of fire, which can reach 109 yards (100 meters) in height. Molten rock can also come out as house-sized lava bombs, little stones called "lapilli," or clouds of ash and dust.

True or False?
Lava has skin.

Answer: **True**
Pahoehoe (pa-hoy-hoy) is a very hot, fluid type of lava that grows a smooth skin on top as it cools. The hot flow continues underneath, even though the crust may be hard enough to walk across.

Can you find five lava bombs?

 Warning: adult help needed!
Make an eruption! Half-fill a jar with baking soda. Cut a circle out of cardstock. Make a slit to the middle and tape into a cone shape. Cut a hole at the top of the cone and place over the jar. Add some red food coloring to vinegar. Pour it into the jar, then stand back! This can be messy: Wear old clothes and do it outdoors!

SPITTING ASH

Violent volcanoes blast out ash and gas. The force of Mount St. Helens' eruption in 1980 was as powerful as 500 atomic bombs going off. The cloud gave amazing red sunsets, and ash fell as far as 745 miles (1,200 kilometers) away in Colorado.

Ash clouds can block out the sun for days. In 1973, the cloud from an eruption on Heimaey (right), off Iceland, left behind a thick blanket of black ash. In some places the ash was over 19 feet (6 meters) deep.

True or False?
There really is a blue moon.

Answer: **True**

Floating clouds of volcanic ash do strange things to light. They can even make the moon and sun seem to glow blue or green!

The static in an ash cloud can also make lightning. To make static, put a metal tray on a plastic bag. Fix a modeling clay "handle" on the tray, then rub it around on the bag. Lift the tray and, with your other hand, touch its edge with a metal fork to see sparks fly!

TIME FREEZER

Ash from volcanoes can freeze people in time! In 79 AD, Mount Vesuvius split open and a huge, glowing cloud billowed out. Over 2,000 people in Pompeii were buried in the blizzard of ash.

Pliny the Elder died in the eruption. His nephew wrote about the event—that's how we know about what happened.

Can you find the bowl of figs?

Pompeii lay forgotten for 1,600 years. Another eruption uncovered the original town. The bodies had decayed leaving people-shaped holes in the hardened ash. By filling these molds with plaster of paris, archaeologists made molds of the Romans—and their pets!

MAKING WAVES

Erupting volcanoes can start tidal waves or tsunamis up to 100 feet (30 meters) high. After the biggest-ever volcanic eruption, at Krakatoa, 36,000 people drowned in huge black walls of water.

Can you find four palm trees?

 True or False?
Tsunamis are always caused by volcanoes.

Answer: **False**
Tsunamis happen after earthquakes, too. Tsunamis following the Chilean earthquake in 1960 were so powerful they toppled the statues on Easter Island.

The steamer Berouw (above) was pitched a mile and a half (2.6 kilometers) upriver by the Krakatoa tsunami in 1883. It is still there today.

The artist Hokusai painted a very famous picture of a tsunami. Called "The Great Wave," it shows an enormous tsunami in front of the Japanese volcano Mount Fujiyama, which is actually over 12,000 feet (3,776 meters) high.

ISLAND BUILDERS

If enough lava builds around an underwater volcano, it will stick out of the sea, making an island. This is how the island of Surtsey was formed in the Icelandic Sea. Surtsey appeared in 1963. By 1968, it measured over a mile (1.9 kilometers) across.

Can you find three Fulmars?

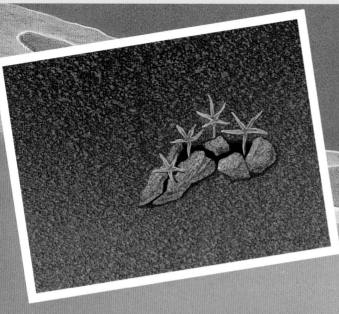

By 1970, a Fulmar had nested on Surtsey, and soon flowers took root. Their seeds were carried from Iceland in bird droppings.

Iceland is a land of fire and ice, with several active volcanoes and geysers. It formed over millions of years from volcanic eruptions in the Mid-Atlantic Ridge. It is over 50,000 times bigger than Surtsey.

UNDERWATER SMOKERS

The seabed surrounding an underwater volcano is an amazing place. Black smokers are formed when hot springs on the seabed gush out water that is black with metals. The metals harden in the cold water, forming tall chimneys.

The world's longest mountain range is the Mid-Atlantic Ridge, a string of volcanoes under water. Submersibles, such as *Alvin*, go down and take photographs of it.

Alvin

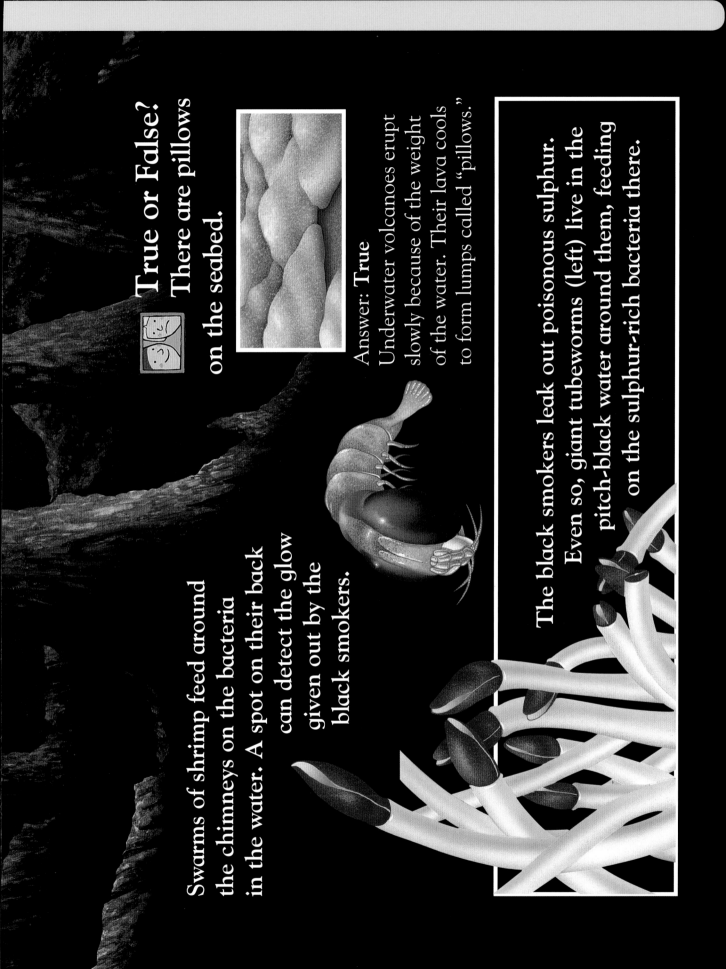

True or False?
There are pillows on the sedbed.

Answer: True
Underwater volcanoes erupt slowly because of the weight of the water. Their lava cools to form lumps called "pillows."

Swarms of shrimp feed around the chimneys on the bacteria in the water. A spot on their back can detect the glow given out by the black smokers.

The black smokers leak out poisonous sulphur. Even so, giant tubeworms (left) live in the pitch-black water around them, feeding on the sulphur-rich bacteria there.

MUD BATH

Some people like taking baths in mud! Volcanic heat underground can cause hot springs and bubbling mud pools. Though some pools are boiling hot and would scald your skin, others are cool enough to bathe in. People wallow in the warm mud. The minerals in the mud leave skin feeling soft and smooth.

The Japanese town of Beppu had 4,000 hot springs all to itself. The Jungle Bath (above), at over 7,100 square yards (6,000 square meters), is the biggest spa in the world.

True or False?
Volcanoes have healing powers.

Answer: **True**

It can't be proven, but lots of people believe they do! In Japan, people like to get up to their necks in warm volcanic sand (left). They believe it can cure illnesses. Drinking mineral-rich water from hot springs is thought to keep the body healthy, and bathing in hot springs soothes pain.

Can you find the swimming cap?

SLEEPING MOUNTAINS

Between eruptions, volcanoes sleep, or are dormant. Sometimes they are dormant for centuries. In France, there are remains of extinct volcanoes. The cone weathers away, but the hard vent remains. It is hard to be sure a volcano is really extinct.

Nogorongoro, an extinct volcano in Tanzania (bottom), is home to flamingoes and hippos. Its crater is a lake, and the lush grassland around it feeds rhinos and zebras.

 ## True or False?
Volcanoes make money.

Answer: **True**
They provide us with precious and useful minerals, which formed millions of years ago in the hardening lava. The South African diamond mine (right) at Kimberley is on the site of an extinct volcano.

Two volcanoes that erupted in Turkey eight million years ago have long disappeared, but the lava left behind a "city" of fairytale cones into which people dug houses and churches that can still be seen today.

SPACE VOLCANOES

Our planet is not the only place where volcanoes are found. One of Jupiter's moons, Io, is covered in erupting volcanoes. The two *Voyager* spacecrafts sent back photographs of the volcanic gas plumes there, which were higher than 30 Mount Everests!

 True or False?

The largest volcano is in space.

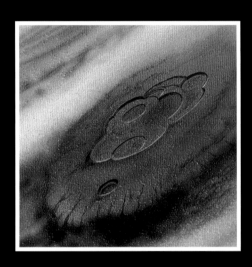

Answer: **True**
The largest known volcano isn't on Earth at all! Mars is home to Olympus Mons, which is 370 miles (600 kilometers) across, and 15 miles (25 kilometers) high. Like all Mars volcanoes, Olympus Mons is extinct.

Nearer to home, there are volcanoes on our Moon, and on Mars and Venus. The *Magellan* spacecraft used radar to take pictures of Venus' volcanoes.

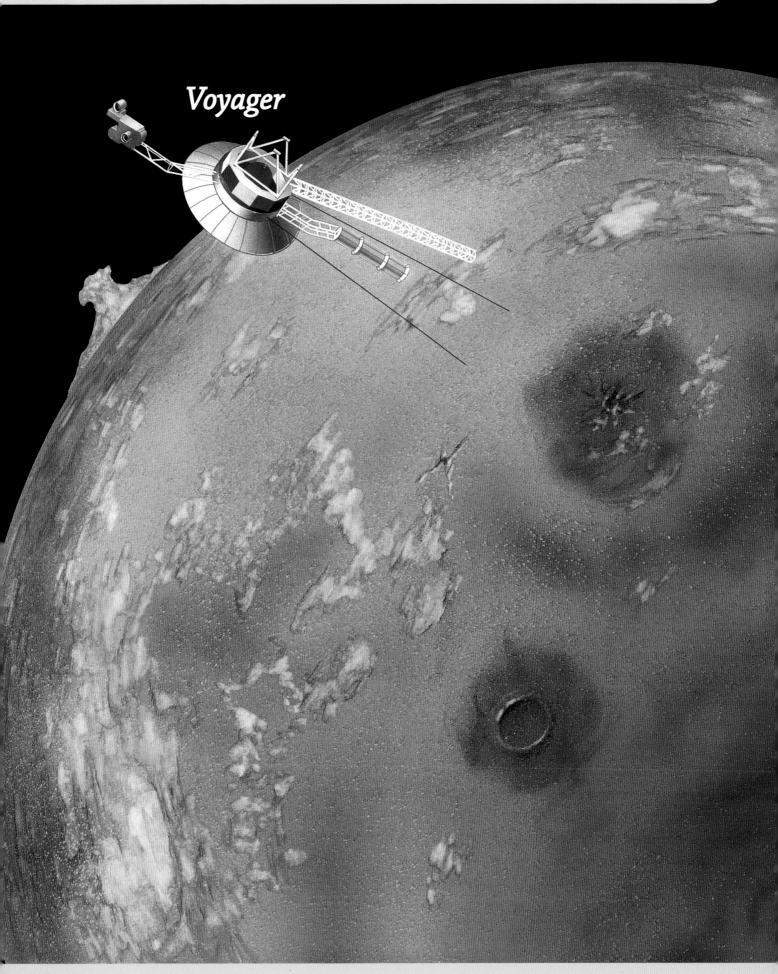

Voyager

HOT WORK

Volcanoes are so hot, the people who study them need special protection. Volcanologists wear special silver clothing, like a space suit, which reflects the heat. Volcanologists can monitor a volcano's activity by taking its temperature and collecting samples.

A compass will not work near a volcano. A volcano has its own magnetic force, which confuses the compass and makes it go berserk. Hold a magnet next to a compass and see what happens.

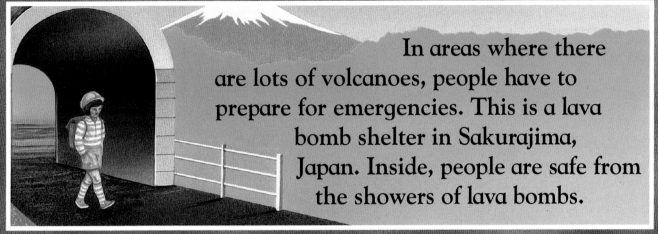

In areas where there are lots of volcanoes, people have to prepare for emergencies. This is a lava bomb shelter in Sakurajima, Japan. Inside, people are safe from the showers of lava bombs.

Volcanologists take samples of lava to examine in the laboratory. They swirl a long pole into the flow to collect it—just like cotton candy collects around a wooden stick.

Volcanologists wear gas masks so they don't breathe in poisonous gases, or choke on ash. Finding out about volcanoes is a dangerous job. When volcanologists can forecast eruptions, they can save lives.

GLOSSARY

Black smoker
A hot spring on the ocean bed.

Caldera
A huge volcanic crater, formed when the slopes of a volcano collapse into the empty magma chamber.

Cone
The "mountain" of hardened lava that builds up around a volcano.

Core
The center of the Earth.

Crater
The bowl-shaped

hollow at the top of a volcano, above the vent.

Crust
The outer layer of the Earth.

Dormant
A volcano is dormant, or sleeping, between eruptions.

Eruption

The way a volcano throws out gases, rocks, and ash on the Earth's surface.

Extinct

A volcano is extinct when it is never going to erupt again.

Fault line

A crack in the Earth's crust.

Geyser

A fountain of water heated by volcanic activity underground.

Lava

Magma that has reached the Earth's surface. It cools as it flows on land or pillows under the sea.

Magma

Hot molten rock, which is still below the Earth's surface.

Mantle

The hot layer of earth between the Earth's crust and Earth's core.

Plates

Large sections of the Earth's crust, which are constantly moving against each other.

Tsunami

A giant wave, caused by a volcanic eruption or an earthquake.

Volcanologist

Someone who studies volcanoes.

INDEX